Little People, BIG DREAMS®
LEONARDO DA VINCI

Written by
Maria Isabel Sánchez Vegara

Illustrated by
Ana Albero

Frances Lincoln
Children's Books

A long time ago, there was a boy named Leonardo who lived in the town of Vinci, near the city of Florence, in Italy. His mind was always full of questions, like how a bat could stay in the air or what made a star glow.

Raised by his grandfather Antonio and his uncle Francesco, Leonardo didn't go to a regular school but learnt freely at home. He loved drawing everything around him to understand it better, and he was really good at it.

Leonardo loved animals and plants as much as he loved sketching them. He drew twisted trees, wildflowers and the way cats curled up to sleep. At the market, he bought caged birds just to set them free and watch them fly into the sky.

Around the age of twelve, he joined other young artists in a workshop run by the great Andrea del Verrocchio, in Florence. There, Leonardo learnt to paint, sculpt and make bright colour powders by crushing plants and stones.

He spent ten years with his teacher, working on many of his artworks. One day, Leonardo painted the face and hair of an angel with such skill that – people said – Verrocchio put down his brush, feeling he couldn't match his pupil's talent.

Yet Leonardo wasn't only drawn to beauty – he was a scientist, too. Understanding how the body worked became a lifelong passion. After leaving Florence, he moved to Milan, where he drew bones and muscles with care.

Leonardo kept notebooks full of detailed drawings and bright ideas about inventions to make people's lives easier. He wrote backwards – perhaps because, as a left-handed writer, it kept the ink from smudging and staining his sleeve.

In Milan, Leonardo worked on a huge religious painting: *The Last Supper*. It showed a long table with thirteen people, all pointing, whispering or reaching across their plates. It was the most alive painting anyone had ever seen.

Still, his most famous masterpiece wasn't that large mural but a smaller painting called *Mona Lisa*, of a lady with a quiet smile. Leonardo carried it from place to place, adding tiny touches of paint here and there, always smiling back at her.

From dukes to queens, everyone was amazed by Leonardo!
He created artworks for walls, chapels and festivals.

As his fame grew, young artists came to learn from the great master. One of them, Francesco, became as close as family.

One day, Leonardo received a special request: to create something extraordinary for a royal celebration. So he built a mechanical lion with a heart full of lilies that walked across the room and surprised the King of France.

His Majesty was so impressed by Leonardo's genius that he invited him to live near his palace in France. From his new home, Leonardo continued working, thinking and dreaming, while his ideas began to travel far beyond time and place . . .

Hundreds of years later, the world is still learning from the questions little Leonardo asked. Through his paintings, notebooks and inventions, he showed us that trying to understand the world is its own kind of joy.

LEONARDO DA VINCI

(Born 1452 – Died 1519)

c.1470

c.1483–87

Leonardo was born in 1452 near the town of Vinci in Italy. His name 'da Vinci' means 'from Vinci'. Leonardo lived a long time ago so we can't be sure what he looked like. The portraits you see above are thought to be of Leonardo, but we'll never know for certain. At the time Leonardo lived, Europe was going through a period of change called the Renaissance. It was an exciting age of new ideas, scientific discoveries and great art. When he was around twelve, Leonardo moved to the city of Florence to become an apprentice in the workshop of the artist Andrea del Verrocchio. There, he learnt how to make things with his hands: painting, sculpting and working with metal. Around 1482, he began working as an artist and engineer for the Duke of Milan. Leonardo was interested in so many

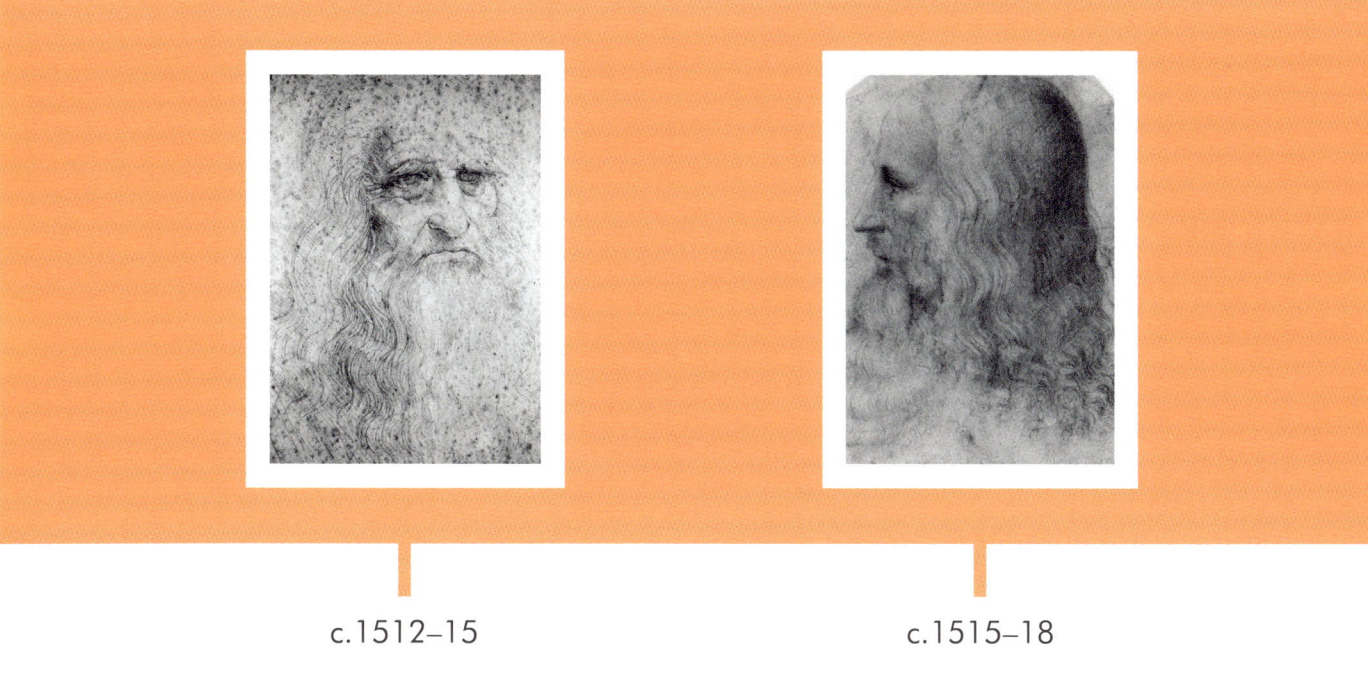

c.1512–15   c.1515–18

different things that he didn't always finish everything he started. One of the works he did complete was the *Last Supper*, a huge wall painting for a monastery. Back in Florence a few years later, he began work on another masterpiece: the *Mona Lisa*. In his thirties he began keeping notebooks filled with sketches, observations and ideas. There were designs for imaginary cities and extraordinary machines, detailed drawings of the human body and investigations into the science of flight. Leonardo even drew up plans for a flying machine, hundreds of years before they were invented! He kept writing and sketching in his notebooks his whole life. Leonardo died aged sixty-seven and spent his last years working for the French king. Today he is remembered as one of the greatest creators in history.

Want to find out more about **Leonardo da Vinci?**
Have a read of this great book:
The Extraordinary Ideas of Leonardo da Vinci by Alex Woolf

Text © 2026 Maria Isabel Sánchez Vegara. Illustrations © 2026 Ana Albero.
Original idea of the series by Maria Isabel Sánchez Vegara, published by Alba Editorial, S.L.U
"Little People, BIG DREAMS" and "Pequeña & Grande" are trademarks of
Alba Editorial S.L.U. and/or Beautifool Couple S.L.
First Published in the UK in 2026 by Frances Lincoln Children's Books, an imprint of The Quarto Group.
1 Triptych Place, London, SE1 9SH, United Kingdom. T 020 7700 6700 **www.Quarto.com**
EEA Representation, WTS Tax d.o.o., Žanova ulica 3, 4000 Kranj, Slovenia. www.wts-tax.si
All rights reserved.
No part of this publication may be reproduced, stored in a retrieval system, or transmitted, in any form,
or by any means, electrical, mechanical, photocopying, recording or otherwise without the prior written
permission of the publisher or a licence permitting restricted copying.

This book is not authorized, licensed or approved by the estate of Leonardo da Vinci.
Any faults are the publisher's who will be happy to rectify for future printings.
A catalogue record for this book is available from the British Library.
ISBN 978-1-80570-186-6
Set in Futura BT.

With scientific consultation by Dr Francesca Borgo, University of St Andrews

Published by Juliet Matthews · Designed by Sasha Moxon, Izzy Bowman and Karissa Santos
Edited by Lucy Menzies and Claire Grace · Editorial management by Izzie Hewitt
Production by Robin Boothroyd
Manufactured in Bosnia and Herzegovina
1 3 5 7 9 8 6 4 2

Photographic acknowledgements (pages 28-29, from left to right): 1. David Victorious over Goliath, circa 1470. Found in the Collection of Museo del Bargello, Firenze. (Photo by Fine Art Images/Heritage Images via Getty Images.) 2. Leonardo da Vinci, Portrait of a Musician, painting in oil on panel. 1483 – 1487, incamerastock, ICP, Alamy. 3. Self-Portrait by Leonardo da Vinci. (Inv. 15571, Coll. Dis. It. I/30.) (Photo by DeAgostini/Getty Images.) 4. Portrait of Leonardo da Vinci, circa 1515 – 1518. Found in the Royal Collection, London. (Photo by Fine Art Images/Heritage Images via Getty Images.)

Collect the Little People, BIG DREAMS® series:

FRIDA KAHLO	COCO CHANEL	MAYA ANGELOU	AMELIA EARHART	AGATHA CHRISTIE	MARIE CURIE	ROSA PARKS	AUDREY HEPBURN	EMMELINE PANKHURST
 ELLA FITZGERALD	ADA LOVELACE	JANE AUSTEN	GEORGIA O'KEEFFE	HARRIET TUBMAN	ANNE FRANK	MOTHER TERESA	JOSEPHINE BAKER	L. M. MONTGOMERY
JANE GOODALL	SIMONE DE BEAUVOIR	MUHAMMAD ALI	STEPHEN HAWKING	MARIA MONTESSORI	VIVIENNE WESTWOOD	MAHATMA GANDHI	DAVID BOWIE	WILMA RUDOLPH
 DOLLY PARTON	BRUCE LEE	RUDOLF NUREYEV	ZAHA HADID	MARY SHELLEY	MARTIN LUTHER KING JR.	DAVID ATTENBOROUGH	ASTRID LINDGREN	EVONNE GOOLAGONG
BOB DYLAN	ALAN TURING	BILLIE JEAN KING	GRETA THUNBERG	JESSE OWENS	JEAN-MICHEL BASQUIAT	ARETHA FRANKLIN	CORAZON AQUINO	PELÉ
 ERNEST SHACKLETON	STEVE JOBS	AYRTON SENNA	LOUISE BOURGEOIS	ELTON JOHN	JOHN LENNON	PRINCE	CHARLES DARWIN	CAPTAIN TOM MOORE
HANS CHRISTIAN ANDERSEN	STEVIE WONDER	MEGAN RAPINOE	MARY ANNING	MALALA YOUSAFZAI	ANDY WARHOL	RUPAUL	MICHELLE OBAMA	MINDY KALING
IRIS APFEL	ROSALIND FRANKLIN	RUTH BADER GINSBURG	MARILYN MONROE	KAMALA HARRIS	ALBERT EINSTEIN	CHARLES DICKENS	YOKO ONO	MICHAEL JORDAN